YOU KNOW
E-MAIL ADD

Louise McKay

SUMMERSDALE

Summersdale Publishers Ltd
46 West Street
Chichester
PO19 1RP
UK

www.summersdale.com

ISBN 1 84024 263 9

Printed and bound in Great Britain

Cartoons by Kate Taylor

YOU KNOW YOU'RE AN E-MAIL ADDICT WHEN . . .

You e-mail your prayers every night.

YOU KNOW YOU'RE AN E-MAIL ADDICT WHEN . . .

You never have any facial expressions beyond those that can be shown by emoticons.

YOU KNOW YOU'RE AN E-MAIL ADDICT WHEN . . .

You take your 'laptop' quite literally and have it surgically implanted into your lap…but when swimming it limits you to the toddler's pool, which is only knee-deep.

YOU KNOW YOU'RE AN E-MAIL ADDICT WHEN . . .

You can type with your toes…and what's more you do. That way you can type two e-mails at the same time.

YOU KNOW YOU'RE AN E-MAIL ADDICT WHEN . . .

YOU KNOW YOU'RE AN E-MAIL ADDICT WHEN . . .

You've long forgotten what a pen looks like.

YOU KNOW YOU'RE AN E-MAIL ADDICT WHEN . . .

You turn down a free luxury cruise when you discover there's no modem port in your cabin.

YOU KNOW YOU'RE AN E-MAIL ADDICT WHEN . . .

You have no idea what any of your mates actually look like. You only recognise them by the prefix of their e-mail address.

YOU KNOW YOU'RE AN E-MAIL ADDICT WHEN . . .

You read to your kids each night. Your favourite kids' book? The C@ in the H@.

YOU KNOW YOU'RE AN E-MAIL ADDICT WHEN . . .

Your poor mother was horrified at your birth to discover a modem lead where the umbilical cord should've been.

YOU KNOW YOU'RE AN E-MAIL ADDICT WHEN . . .

You sue your parents for conceiving you before e-mail was around – just think what you missed as a baby.

YOU KNOW YOU'RE AN E-MAIL ADDICT WHEN . . .

You have a keyboard designed for your cat, so he can e-mail you when he wants feeding. Not surprisingly, he's starved to death.

YOU KNOW YOU'RE AN E-MAIL ADDICT WHEN . . .

YOU KNOW YOU'RE AN E-MAIL ADDICT WHEN . . .

You were one of the only people who bought and actually used a WAP phone.

YOU KNOW YOU'RE AN E-MAIL ADDICT WHEN . . .

You have a recurring nightmare about being reincarnated into a fish. How on earth could you type with gills?

YOU KNOW YOU'RE AN E-MAIL ADDICT WHEN . . .

Your middle name is @.

YOU KNOW YOU'RE AN E-MAIL ADDICT WHEN . . .

You dream in http.

YOU KNOW YOU'RE AN E-MAIL ADDICT WHEN . . .

You even talk in trendy lowercase… when you talk, that is.

YOU KNOW YOU'RE AN E-MAIL ADDICT WHEN . . .

You'd rather e-mail the emergency services than dial 999 when your house is burning down. They arrive a week later to find a charred body sitting at a keyboard.

YOU KNOW YOU'RE AN E-MAIL ADDICT WHEN . . .

You put your girlfriend off sex forever. Hardly surprising as you kept on asking her to open her *Inbox* for you.

YOU KNOW YOU'RE AN E-MAIL ADDICT WHEN . . .

YOU KNOW YOU'RE AN E-MAIL ADDICT WHEN . . .

You love the traditions of Christmas: helping your kids e-mail their letters to Santa Claus.

YOU KNOW YOU'RE AN E-MAIL ADDICT WHEN . . .

Your partner complains incessantly about your irritating habit of getting up in the middle of the night…for a forward slash.

YOU KNOW YOU'RE AN E-MAIL ADDICT WHEN . . .

You suffer from a bad case of cold turkey when your Internet connection fails for a whole day.

YOU KNOW YOU'RE AN E-MAIL ADDICT WHEN . . .

YOU KNOW YOU'RE AN E-MAIL ADDICT WHEN . . .

You have shares in the company that makes wrist splints for RSI sufferers.

YOU KNOW YOU'RE AN E-MAIL ADDICT WHEN . . .

Your dream woman is AOL's Connie. That see-through dress really gets you going.

YOU KNOW YOU'RE AN E-MAIL ADDICT WHEN . . .

The first thing you do in the morning is shower, shave and download.

YOU KNOW YOU'RE AN E-MAIL ADDICT WHEN . . .

YOU KNOW YOU'RE AN E-MAIL ADDICT WHEN . . .

You fully advocate sex before marriage, as long as it's carried out online.

YOU KNOW YOU'RE AN E-MAIL ADDICT WHEN . . .

Your favourite film is *You've Got Mail.* If only Hollywood would produce more e-mail related films instead of stories with action, adventure and good plots.

YOU KNOW YOU'RE AN E-MAIL ADDICT WHEN . . .

Your outlook on life is quite simple: *Outlook Express*.

YOU KNOW YOU'RE AN E-MAIL ADDICT WHEN . . .

You read (and actually laugh out loud at) all those jokes that circulate via e-mail.

YOU KNOW YOU'RE AN E-MAIL ADDICT WHEN . . .

You've been married more times than Joan Collins but never actually met any of your spouses. Isn't the Internet great?

YOU KNOW YOU'RE AN E-MAIL ADDICT WHEN . . .

When you're diagnosed with sciatica, you download *Disc Doctor* software and expect to make a speedy recovery.

YOU KNOW YOU'RE AN E-MAIL ADDICT WHEN . . .

Your first word was *modem*...and that was only last week.

YOU KNOW YOU'RE AN E-MAIL ADDICT WHEN . . .

YOU KNOW YOU'RE AN E-MAIL ADDICT WHEN . . .

The only attachments you're likely to form in life are on your computer.

YOU KNOW YOU'RE AN E-MAIL ADDICT WHEN . . .

You refer to sleep as *working offline*.

YOU KNOW YOU'RE AN E-MAIL ADDICT WHEN . . .

The only true connection you've ever made is…with your computer server.

YOU KNOW YOU'RE AN E-MAIL ADDICT WHEN . . .

You like to vet people before forming a friendship…by clicking on 'properties'.

YOU KNOW YOU'RE AN E-MAIL ADDICT WHEN . . .

Your favourite food is spam.

YOU KNOW YOU'RE AN E-MAIL ADDICT WHEN . . .

Your dominant hand has become clawed because you haven't let go of your Palm Pilot since you bought it. That wasn't a problem until you realised you could no longer indulge in your other hobby.

YOU KNOW YOU'RE AN E-MAIL ADDICT WHEN . . .

You count new messages, not sheep.

YOU KNOW YOU'RE AN E-MAIL ADDICT WHEN . . .

YOU KNOW YOU'RE AN E-MAIL ADDICT WHEN . . .

You take up celebrity stalking when you realise that it's possible to do so without leaving your desk. What you don't realise is that Scotland Yard has e-mail too.

YOU KNOW YOU'RE AN E-MAIL ADDICT WHEN . . .

You think postmen are an anachronism.

YOU KNOW YOU'RE AN E-MAIL ADDICT WHEN . . .

You watch *Pop Idol* and are bitterly disappointed that POP3 doesn't get a look in.

YOU KNOW YOU'RE AN E-MAIL ADDICT WHEN . . .

Your boss at work gives you a bollocking and you apologise by explaining that 'some errors occurred while processing the requested tasks'.

YOU KNOW YOU'RE AN E-MAIL ADDICT WHEN . . .

You fall into a clinical depression when you see 'no new messages' appear on your screen.

YOU KNOW YOU'RE AN E-MAIL ADDICT WHEN . . .

You open countless *Hotmail* accounts just for the thrill of receiving junk a hundred times over.

YOU KNOW YOU'RE AN E-MAIL ADDICT WHEN . . .

You're a sensitive little flower, so when you dump your lover by e-mail at least you do it in lower case.

YOU KNOW YOU'RE AN E-MAIL ADDICT WHEN . . .

YOU KNOW YOU'RE AN E-MAIL ADDICT WHEN . . .

Your life has never been so meaningful.

YOU KNOW YOU'RE AN E-MAIL ADDICT WHEN . . .

You report your boyfriend to the police for aggressive behaviour. EVERYONE KNOWS IT'S BAD TO USE CAPITAL LETTERS IN AN E-MAIL.

YOU KNOW YOU'RE AN E-MAIL ADDICT WHEN . . .

You keep your balls immaculately clean…but the other parts of your mice are quite grubby from overuse.

YOU KNOW YOU'RE AN E-MAIL ADDICT WHEN . . .

You'd rather have a flat-screened monitor than a flat stomach.

YOU KNOW YOU'RE AN E-MAIL ADDICT WHEN . . .

You sold your letterbox to raise more cash for a new PDA.

YOU KNOW YOU'RE AN E-MAIL ADDICT WHEN . . .

You're looking for a man who doesn't just hang-up after sex.

YOU KNOW YOU'RE AN E-MAIL ADDICT WHEN . . .

Your best chat-up line is 'I could be your service provider'.

YOU KNOW YOU'RE AN E-MAIL ADDICT WHEN . . .

YOU KNOW YOU'RE AN E-MAIL ADDICT WHEN . . .

You believe the greatest icon of the 21st century is 'Incoming Mail'.

YOU KNOW YOU'RE AN E-MAIL ADDICT WHEN . . .

Your idea of *Viagra* is something that will maintain your e-mail connection for longer.

YOU KNOW YOU'RE AN E-MAIL ADDICT WHEN . . .

In the throes of passion, you accidentally press *delete*. Damn, maybe your mum was right when she advised you to date the normal way.

YOU KNOW YOU'RE AN E-MAIL ADDICT WHEN . . .

The most romantic thing you've ever done is use proper punctuation…to show that you care.

YOU KNOW YOU'RE AN E-MAIL ADDICT WHEN . . .

You plan to send your daughters to a Swiss finishing school…to learn the necessary netiquette befitting young girls of today.

YOU KNOW YOU'RE AN E-MAIL ADDICT WHEN . . .

YOU KNOW YOU'RE AN E-MAIL ADDICT WHEN . . .

You fantasise about being covered in love-bytes.

YOU KNOW YOU'RE AN E-MAIL ADDICT WHEN . . .

Your e-mail address book is the only proof that you actually have any mates.

YOU KNOW YOU'RE AN E-MAIL ADDICT WHEN . . .

You put your computer on a waiting list for the MMR jab…after all, some viruses can be fatal.

YOU KNOW YOU'RE AN E-MAIL ADDICT WHEN . . .

At least half of your day is spent circulating e-mail chain letters to ten people within the next minutes. You always fall for that shit.

YOU KNOW YOU'RE AN E-MAIL ADDICT WHEN . . .

Your first date was spent in an Internet Café.

YOU KNOW YOU'RE AN E-MAIL ADDICT WHEN . . .

YOU KNOW YOU'RE AN E-MAIL ADDICT WHEN . . .

ADSL gets you so excited that you hold a party…online in order to show-off your new, super-fast connection.

YOU KNOW YOU'RE AN E-MAIL ADDICT WHEN . . .

You actually know what SMTP stands for.

YOU KNOW YOU'RE AN E-MAIL ADDICT WHEN . . .

Sometimes you set up a *holiday reply*, just so people think you lead a normal life. Little do they know you're sitting at home and using another e-mail account. You freak ;-)

YOU KNOW YOU'RE AN E-MAIL ADDICT WHEN . . .

Your idea of relaxation is creating folders to subdivide your messages.

YOU KNOW YOU'RE AN E-MAIL ADDICT WHEN . . .

You venture to a shop for the first time ever, buy something with your credit card and give them your URL and a thought for the day when they ask for your *signature*.

YOU KNOW YOU'RE AN E-MAIL ADDICT WHEN . . .

You are terribly snobby. You only talk to *.coms* and *.co.uks* – *.nets* are **so** last year.

YOU KNOW YOU'RE AN E-MAIL ADDICT WHEN . . .

You are having difficulty choosing a domain name for your newborn baby.

YOU KNOW YOU'RE AN E-MAIL ADDICT WHEN . . .

YOU KNOW YOU'RE AN E-MAIL ADDICT WHEN . . .

Your aunt phones to check your address before she sends you a birthday present. You give her your e-mail address and tell her to send it as an attachment.

YOU KNOW YOU'RE AN E-MAIL ADDICT WHEN . . .

Your agree to join E-mail Addicts Anonymous and everyone is thrilled to hear that you are receiving support from a buddy – until you introduce them…to *CompuServe*.

YOU KNOW YOU'RE AN E-MAIL ADDICT WHEN . . .

You have invented a new speech impediment...you talk with an *ISP*.

YOU KNOW YOU'RE AN E-MAIL ADDICT WHEN . . .

You are chuffed when your kids ask for a mouse for Christmas but you can't understand their disappointment at receiving brand new cordless ones from *Microsoft*.

YOU KNOW YOU'RE AN E-MAIL ADDICT WHEN . . .

On a first date it's vital to perform a system security check… by seeing what sort of bra she's wearing.

YOU KNOW YOU'RE AN E-MAIL ADDICT WHEN . . .

Your online doctor has put you on a diet: no cookies.

YOU KNOW YOU'RE AN E-MAIL ADDICT WHEN . . .

You're not in contact with your parents…because they can't get the hang of e-mail.

YOU KNOW YOU'RE AN E-MAIL ADDICT WHEN . . .

YOU KNOW YOU'RE AN E-MAIL ADDICT WHEN . . .

You terminate relationships by clicking on *block sender*.

YOU KNOW YOU'RE AN E-MAIL ADDICT WHEN . . .

YCIA: You communicate in acronyms.
(Work this one out: YAASF)

YOU KNOW YOU'RE AN E-MAIL ADDICT WHEN . . .

Your ideal holiday is a two-week trip to *Silicon Valley*.

YOU KNOW YOU'RE AN E-MAIL ADDICT WHEN . . .

YOU KNOW YOU'RE AN E-MAIL ADDICT WHEN . . .

You commission a portrait of yourself and are impressed at the great likeness:
: — D

YOU KNOW YOU'RE AN E-MAIL ADDICT WHEN . . .

YOU KNOW YOU'RE AN E-MAIL ADDICT WHEN . . .

At parties, you introduce yourself by verifying your username and password.

YOU KNOW YOU'RE AN E-MAIL ADDICT WHEN . . .

You've never used the Shift key on your keyboard because you've never needed to type a capital letter.

YOU KNOW YOU'RE AN E-MAIL ADDICT WHEN . . .

You are always flattered when people refer to you as a nerd.

YOU KNOW YOU'RE AN E-MAIL ADDICT WHEN . . .

YOU KNOW YOU'RE AN E-MAIL ADDICT WHEN . . .

You conduct e-mail conversations with your friends at work that go on all day, and most of the messages consist of only one or two words: 'did he?' 'really?' 'how big?' etc. One short phone call would have replaced those 75 messages.

YOU KNOW YOU'RE AN E-MAIL ADDICT WHEN . . .

You have renamed yourself by deed poll to WYSIWYG, but only you get the joke.

YOU KNOW YOU'RE AN E-MAIL ADDICT WHEN . . .

Housework to you means emptying your 'deleted items' folder.

YOU KNOW YOU'RE AN E-MAIL ADDICT WHEN . . .

Your computer crashes but pouring vials of *Rescue Remedy* over the hard drive doesn't help.

YOU KNOW YOU'RE AN E-MAIL ADDICT WHEN . . .

Your eyes light up when people suggest that Bill Gates is going for World domination.

YOU KNOW YOU'RE AN E-MAIL ADDICT WHEN . . .

YOU KNOW YOU'RE AN E-MAIL ADDICT WHEN . . .

You make *Excite* and *Yahoo* joint executors of your will.

YOU KNOW YOU'RE AN E-MAIL ADDICT WHEN . . .

You think properly spelled and grammaticised text looks like a foreign language.

YOU KNOW YOU'RE AN E-MAIL ADDICT WHEN . . .

On those rare occasions when you actually talk, you confuse people by copying them into your conversation.

YOU KNOW YOU'RE AN E-MAIL ADDICT WHEN . . .

And blind copying your guide dog.

YOU KNOW YOU'RE AN E-MAIL ADDICT WHEN . . .

You are the life and soul of the party…as long as it's being held in a chat room.

YOU KNOW YOU'RE AN E-MAIL ADDICT WHEN . . .

YOU KNOW YOU'RE AN E-MAIL ADDICT WHEN . . .

Your boss is really pleased with you: whenever she walks past your desk you are always so busy typing…and with a smile on your face too.

YOU KNOW YOU'RE AN E-MAIL ADDICT WHEN . . .

You have a massive collection of art…clip art, that is.

YOU KNOW YOU'RE AN E-MAIL ADDICT WHEN . . .

Your phone bill would be in the Guinness Book of Records…but it takes up too much space.

YOU KNOW YOU'RE AN E-MAIL ADDICT WHEN . . .

YOU KNOW YOU'RE AN E-MAIL ADDICT WHEN . . .

You have more open windows than a double-glazing salesman does.

YOU KNOW YOU'RE AN E-MAIL ADDICT WHEN . . .

You reply to an invitation to a royal garden party with an e-mail that begins 'hi . . .' and contains no punctuation.

YOU KNOW YOU'RE AN E-MAIL ADDICT WHEN . . .

You think grammar is a measure of weight.

YOU KNOW YOU'RE AN E-MAIL ADDICT WHEN . . .

On your CV you cite 'communication' as a skill but at job interviews employers are surprised to find that you can't actually speak.

YOU KNOW YOU'RE AN E-MAIL ADDICT WHEN . . .

You lose both arms in a freak e-mail accident but teach yourself to communicate online with other bodily protuberances.

YOU KNOW YOU'RE AN E-MAIL ADDICT WHEN . . .

The Discovery Channel features a full-length documentary about you and receives viewer complaints, as no one actually believes that anyone could use e-mail as you do.

YOU KNOW YOU'RE AN E-MAIL ADDICT WHEN . . .

Your passport states that your distinguishing features are your exceptionally large outbox and your interesting assortment of drafts.

YOU KNOW YOU'RE AN E-MAIL ADDICT WHEN . . .

You come across as a bit of a tw@. <J>

YOU KNOW YOU'RE AN E-MAIL ADDICT WHEN . . .

You don't read the papers: you think creating a *newsgroup* will keep you up-to-date with affairs instead…but all you seem to receive is information on the latest porn films.

YOU KNOW YOU'RE AN E-MAIL ADDICT WHEN . . .

Your friends don't bat an eyelid when you call your baby girl *Eudora* but they start to show concern when you name your second child *Lotus Notes*.